FAMILY HOME EVENINGS

FOR DADS

by
Dianne Friden
Carolyn Siemers
Barbara Thackeray

Fourth Printing: February, 2003

International Standard Book Number:
0-88290-673-9

Horizon Publishers' Catalog and Order Number:
1257

Printed and distributed
in the United States of America by

**Horizon
Publishers**
& Distributors, Incorporated

Mailing Address:
P.O. Box 490
Bountiful, Utah 84011-0490

Street Address:
50 South 500 West
Bountiful, Utah 84010

Local Phone: (801) 295-9451
WATS (toll free): 1 (800) 453-0812
FAX: (801) 295-0196

E-mail: horizonp@burgoyne.com
Internet: http://www.horizonpublishers.com

About the Authors

Dianne Friden

Dianne Friden grew up in Brisbane, Australia where she taught elementary school before moving to Utah and graduating from BYU with a degree in Communications. She married Charles Friden and settled in Northern California where they and four of their eight children still live on their family ranch. Dianne is actively involved in The Church of Jesus Christ of Latter-day Saints where she has served in many capacities. Collaborating on books like this is only one of the interests that keep her life busy in between her family, community and business responsibilities.

Carolyn Siemers

Carolyn Siemers was born and raised in Stockton, California. She attended college in San Jose, California, majoring in Nutrition and Family Life Education. A convert to her church, she and her husband are the only members in their extended families. Carolyn currently resides in a small town in Northern California with her husband Roger and two of their five children. At the time of this writing two of her children have served missions for The Church of Jesus Christ of Latter-day Saints, and Carolyn is excitedly awaiting the arrival of her first grandchild.

Barbara Ann Thackeray

Barbara Ann Thackeray, a native of Fort Jones, California, joined The Church of Jesus Christ of Latter-day Saints at age 19. Since that time she has served in numerous positions in the Church including Primary President, Young Women's and Relief Society Counselor, and Sunday School teacher. When she is not busy taking care of her family and church callings, she enjoys pursuing her other interests which include reading, sewing, and sports. She and her husband Scott are the parents of five children.

The authors have lived in the same community for over twenty years and have worked together on many projects. Their desire is to share more of their creative ideas in ways that will inspire others. They lovingly dedicate this book to their husbands, who are now left without excuse.

Contents

1
TREASURE HUNT

Purpose:

To illustrate that the Book of Mormon is a treasure because it teaches what we must do to be happy.

Planning Ahead:

Decide on a suitable treasure for the hunt. If it isn't food, arrange for or assign refreshments if desired.

Preparation: (last minute)

Copy or tear out the treasure-hunt clues and separate them. Hide each clue appropriately in the house. Choose as many as you like but save one to read to the family to get the hunt started. At the last location hide a Book of Mormon or a set of scriptures. Slip one last paper deep inside its pages so that it will not readily appear. It will be a final clue leading to a treat. Make sure you have something like a rented video or candy hidden appropriately.

Process:

Part A: Opening hymn: "The Iron Rod" (Hymns, page 274); Opening prayer; Scripture: Matthew 6:20, 21.

Part B: Explain to the family that several clues have been hidden around the house. As they find one and read it carefully they should be able to figure out where the next clue is hidden. At the end of the hunt they will find a treasure, which they must bring back to the family room. When they return with the book, ask them why the book is considered a treasure. Explain that we must search the Book of Mormon diligently to find the things that will make us happy. After some discussion, have them search carefully through the book where they will discover the last piece of paper. This will be a final clue. While they are enjoying the second treasure, explain that they would not have enjoyed this if they had not found out about it in the Book of Mormon. The Book of Mormon is a treasure because it shows us how to find the things that will make us happy. Explain that the Book of Mormon will not help us find candy or money, but it will help us find other things that will make our lives happy. Discuss the kinds of things these might be, like: it shows us how to make good decisions, or how we can return to live with Heavenly Father.

Part C: Refreshments; Closing prayer.

Treasure Hunt Clues

Pillow: 2 Nephi 33:3 "For I pray continually for them by day and mine eyes water mine PILLOW by night."

Clock: 2 Nephi 2:3 "behold in the fulness of TIME he cometh to bring salvation unto men."

Cup: Mosiah 3:26 "Therefore, they have drunk out of the CUP of the wrath of God."

Plates: Jacob 1:2 "Write upon these PLATES a few of these things which I have considered to be most precious."

Door: Helaman 8:27 "Behold, it is now even at your DOORS."

Broom: Jacob 5:66 "And thus will I SWEEP away the bad out of my vineyard."

Mother: Mosiah 13:20 "Honor thy father and thy MOTHER."

Windows: 3 Nephi 24:10 "Open you the WINDOWS of heaven."

Scales: 2 Nephi 30:6 "and their SCALES of darkness shall begin to fall from their eyes."

Bed: Mosiah 24:19 "And in the morning the Lord caused a DEEP SLEEP to come upon the Lamanites."

Spoon: Mosiah 11:28 "For he had said these things that he might STIR UP my people to anger one with another."

Pantry: 3 Nephi 24:10 "Bring ye all the tithes into the STORE-HOUSE, that there may be meat in my house."

Sugar: 1 Nephi 8:11 "and I beheld that it was most SWEET, above all that I ever before tasted."

Water Faucet: 1 Nephi 17:29 "And there came forth WATER, that the children of Israel might quench their thirst."

Toothbrush: Mosiah 16:2 "and they shall have cause to howl, and weep, and wail, and gnash their TEETH."

T.V: 2 Nephi 4:23 "And he hath given me knowledge by VISIONS IN THE NIGHT TIME."

Milk: 2 Nephi 9:50 "And he that hath no money, come buy and eat; yea come buy wine and MILK without money and without price."

2
OUTSMART DAD

Purpose:

To illustrate the cunning devices Satan uses.

Planning Ahead:

Pick up a 50-cent candy bar for each family member. Make up some punch in one pitcher. In another, make up a container of water colored with food coloring (or Kool-aid without sugar).

Preparation: (last minute)

Make sure you have a scale or tape measure available.

Process:

Part A: Opening hymn: "Choose the Right" (Hymns, page 239); Opening prayer; Scripture: Moroni 7:16-17.

Part B: Tell the children that they can pay a dollar to try to outsmart Dad. If they have their own dollars, all the better. If not, Mom can give them a dollar each.

Explain that if they pay Dad a dollar he will guess their exact weight to the quarter pound, or height to the quarter inch. If he is wrong, the child will get a candy bar. Be sure to show them the array of candy bars you have purchased. As each child pays Dad a dollar, he makes a guess of the weight or height and then they are measured or weighed. Of course he will have made an incorrect estimate, so will hand over the candy bars. After the gloating is over, explain to the children that in fact Dad did outsmart them because those candy bars cost him 50 cents each, and they paid a dollar for them. They could have taken their dollars to the store and bought 2 candy bars each, instead. Now Dad can buy twice as many candy bars for himself, and they have in fact lost 50 cents!

Compare this to the tactics Satan uses. He makes a situation look like it will be fun or you will be a winner, when in fact you will be a loser. Explain that we must examine the situations we find ourselves in very carefully to avoid being deceived by Satan. Invite the kids over for some punch, but serve the colored water. Uh Oh! were they careful not to be deceived again? After they have tasted it, replace it with the tasty punch!

Part C: Serve candy bars for refreshments; Closing prayer.

3
EGG WALK

Purpose:

To teach the importance of listening to our parents and leaders.

Planning Ahead:

Make sure there is a box of crackers and a dozen eggs in the house. Assign or arrange for refreshments, if desired.

Preparation: (last minute)

Find something to be used as a blindfold.

Process:

Part A: Opening song: "Follow the Prophet" (Children's Songbook, page 110); Opening prayer; Scripture: 1 Nephi 3:7.

Part B: Have the family bring a dozen eggs into the living room. When everyone is seated, scatter the eggs on the floor of the room. Explain that one or two people need to leave the room, take their shoes off, and be blindfolded. Two other people will be chosen as guides. When the blindfolded family members return, they will be led to one end of the room and the guides will give specific directions to help them walk through the room without crushing any eggs. They will give directions like "take a step to the left," or "take a giant step ahead of you." The object will be to see who can safely navigate the room.

After this explanation, proceed by sending the volunteers out of the room. After they have left, have the rest of the family replace the eggs with crackers. When the activity is over, point out how important it is that we listen to the guides in our lives. If we listen and follow their advice we can avoid getting into messy situations. Those messy situations can make things difficult for us (like getting egg all over our feet), and also they can make things difficult for others (like whoever has to clean up the eggs from the carpet). Ask who the guides are that we should listen to as we travel through life. (Our parents, our church leaders and the prophet.)

Part C: Refreshments; Closing prayer.

4
BOOK OF MORMON BASKETBALL

Purpose:

To review the family's knowledge of the Book of Mormon.

Planning Ahead:

Assign or arrange for refreshments, if desired.

Preparation: (last minute)

You will need a bucket, bowl or wastebasket at the end of the room. Set three pieces of masking tape or objects like a broom, a chair and a pillow at various distances from the basket. You will also need a soft ball, a wad of tin foil, or a stuffed animal as a basketball.

Questions for the competition are on page 87-90 at the back of the book.

Process:

Part A: Opening song: "Choose the Right Way" (Children's Songbook, page 160); Opening prayer; Scripture: D&C 130:19.

Part B: Explain that you are going to play Book of Mormon basketball to see how much the family knows about the Book of Mormon. Questions will be asked, and if the answer is correct the team will score 2 points. They will also have the opportunity to increase their score by shooting a basket. They may shoot from any of the three lines. A basket made from one of these lines increases their score by a value of 2, 4, or 6 extra points depending on its distance from the basket. Divide the family into teams and let the game begin!

Part C: Refreshments; Closing prayer.

5
FAMILY PHANTOM

Purpose:

To have some fun doing a service project.

Planning Ahead:

Pick up at least 3 tubes of refrigerated cookie dough on the way home from work. Make sure there are some paper plates and plastic wrap, or even just some tin foil in the house.

Preparation: (last minute)

None.

Process:

Part A: Opening song: "Jesus Said Love Everyone" (Children's Songbook, page 61); Opening prayer; Scripture: Mosiah 23:15.

Part B: Explain that the family is going to bake cookies and take them to some families they would like to surprise. Let the family choose two or three families. If they have trouble choosing, suggest Primary teachers, home teachers or the Bishopric. Follow the directions on the cookie-dough packages, and while they are baking assign some family members to make two or three copies of the Family Phantom poem at the end of the lesson. When the cookies have cooled, place them on a paper plate and wrap them in plastic wrap, or simply wrap up a bundle in tin foil. Attach a poem to each plate. Sneak to the homes of the recipients and deliver the cookies without being caught! Save some cookies for your own family.

Part C: After returning home, enjoy the leftover cookies. Closing prayer.

Family Night Phantom Poem:

SSShhh! Can You Keep A Secret?

There's a family night phantom who's been to your house.

He hopes you didn't hear him, he was quiet as a mouse.

He leaves stories or treats for families to share—

It really doesn't matter—you'll know if he's been there.

He hopes that what he's left tonight will be enjoyed by you.

We're hoping that next family night, you'll be a phantom too!

6
SMILE

Purpose:

To begin or update personal histories.

Planning Ahead:

Calendar this in the Summer. Check the camera for film.

Preparation: (last minute)

None.

Process:

Part A: Opening hymn: "Dearest Children, God is Near You" (Hymns, page 86); Opening prayer; Scripture: Alma 37:2 .

Part B: Have the family get in the car and drive to their schools, their ward meetinghouse, their place of baptism, Grandma's house, or any other place that has played an important role in their lives. Take a photo of each family member outside each appropriate building to record the place in his personal history book. On the way home, stop somewhere for a treat.

Part C: Back at home, call on someone to give the closing prayer.

7
BONKERS

Purpose:

To have fun memorizing the prophets.

Planning Ahead:

Assign or arrange for refreshments.

Preparation: (last minute)

Roll up a sock and stuff it in the toe of another sock.

Process:

Part A: Opening song: "Keep the Commandments" (Children's Songbook, page 146); Opening prayer; Scripture: D&C 1:38.

Part B: Choose a category and have each family member choose a prophet's name from the list following. Sit in a circle and explain the rules to the family. One member (The Bonker) stands in the middle with the stuffed sock. The game begins when one member calls out the name of another prophet in the circle. The Bonker tries to hit over the head the person whose name was called, before he can call out the name of another prophet in the circle.

Part C: Refreshments; Closing prayer.

Some Suggested Prophets' Names

Nephi	Adam	Joseph Smith Jr.
Jacob	Moses	Brigham Young
Enos	Samuel	John Taylor
Mosiah	Job	Wilford Woodruff
Alma	Isaiah	Lorenzo Snow
Helaman	Jeremiah	Joseph F. Smith
Mormon	Ezekiel	Heber J. Grant
Moroni	Daniel	George Albert Smith
Ether	Amos	David O. McKay
	Jonah	Joseph Fielding Smith
	Micah	Harold B. Lee
	Malachi	Spencer W. Kimball
		Ezra Taft Benson
		Howard W. Hunter
		Gordon B. Hinckley

8
FAMILY
BOOK OF RECORDS

Purpose:

To build self esteem.

Planning Ahead:

Assign or arrange for refreshments. Make sure you have whatever is necessary for some of the records. For example: bubble gum, crackers, bucket of blocks.

Preparation: (last minute)

Gather tools for record attempts. For example: find a tape measure and a watch with a second hand. Have pen and paper ready for recording results.

Process:

Part A: Opening hymn: "I Am A Child of God" (Hymns, page 301); Opening Prayer; Scripture: Psalms 82:6.

Part B: Encourage the children to set family records in some of the following categories:

> Building the tallest block tower
> Balancing on one foot for the longest time

Walking around the house blindfolded without bumping into
    anything for the longest time
Blowing the biggest bubble
Staring at someone without giggling for the longest time
Reciting "Twinkle Twinkle Little Star" in the shortest time
Singing the most of "Twinkle, Twinkle, Little Star"
    with a mouth full of crackers without laughing

Place the sheet in a binder or other safe place for future record breaking attempts.

No one can attempt to break someone else's record for at least 24 hours.

Part C: For refreshments, set another record. For example: eating a bowl of ice cream the fastest with a knife. Closing prayer.

9
THE EDGE

Purpose:

To teach the importance of avoiding the evils of today.

Planning Ahead:

Assign or arrange for refreshments.

Preparation: (last minute)

Clear off the kitchen table and get out a salt shaker (preferably plastic).

Process:

Part A: Opening hymn: "Do What Is Right" (Hymns, page 237); Opening prayer; Scripture: D&C 98:11.

Part B: Explain the rules of the game to the family:

Two players sit or stand at opposite ends of the table. One slides the shaker to the other. The object is to come as close to the edge as possible without the shaker going over. If you want to keep score, three slides each makes up one game. You may want to place a blanket or other padding material on the floor underneath each player. After everyone has had as many turns as you see fit, tell the following story:

"There is an oft-told story of three men who applied for the job of driving coaches for a transportation company. The successful applicant would be driving over high, dangerous and precipitous mountain roads. Asked how well he could drive, the first one replied, 'I am a good, experienced driver. I can drive so close to the edge of the precipice that the wide metal tire of the vehicle will skirt the edge and never go off.'

" 'That is good driving,' said the employer.

"The second man boasted, 'Oh, I can do better than that. I can drive so accurately that the tire of the vehicle will lap over, half of the tire on the edge of the precipice, and the other half in the air over the edge.'

"The employer wondered what the third man could offer, and was surprised and pleased to hear, 'Well, sir, I can keep just as far away from the edge as possible.' It is needless to ask which of the men got the job." (Spencer W. Kimball, The Miracle of Forgiveness, pp 217-18.)

Explain that we must be like the third driver and wisely choose to avoid danger. It sometimes may seem like fun to see how close we can get to the edge, but the risk of falling off the edge is too great and could destroy us.

Part C: Refreshments; Closing prayer.

10
WHO AM I?

Purpose:

To learn more about the prophets of old.

Planning Ahead:

Assign or arrange for refreshments. Photocopy the lists of clues from pages 26-30. Cut them apart into complete sets of clues for the various prophets.

Preparation: (last minute)

Gather some bath towels, dish towels, sheets and pins.

Process:

Part A: Opening song: "Stand For the Right" (Children's Songbook Page 159); Opening Prayer; Scripture: Alma 53:21.

Part B: Invite a family member to go out of the room and use the towels, etc. to dress up as an ancient Book of Mormon or Bible prophet. Assign him to be a particular prophet and give him the set of clues for that prophet. When he returns, he will begin to give clues as to his identity. Have the family members guess who the prophet is. Each family member has as many turns as time will allow.

Part C: Refreshments and closing prayer.

Clues For the Prophets

Who Am I?

1. I was an obedient son.

2. I came from Jerusalem.

3. I built a ship for my family to sail to the promised land.

4. The Liahona showed me where to get food for my family.

5. I killed a man once because the Spirit told me to.

6. I got the brass plates from Laban.

7. I had brothers named Laman, Lemuel, Sam, Jacob, and Joseph.

Answer: My name is NEPHI

1. I quoted Isaiah 53.

2. I quoted the Ten Commandments to wicked priests.

3. I was put in prison.

4. I prophesied that the king would be destroyed.

5. I was bound and brought before the king of the land.

6. My preaching converted Alma.

7. I was burned to death.

Answer: My name is ABINADI

1. In my day, the Nephites were wicked and the Lamanites were righteous.

2. I prophesied that before 400 years passed away, the Nephites would be destroyed unless they repented.

3. I was visited by an angel who told me what to tell the Nephites.

4. I preached repentance from high atop a city wall.

6. I prophesied of the signs that would follow
    Jesus Christ's death.

7. Those who didn't believe my preaching threw stones at me.

Answer: My name is SAMUEL

1. I was a Nephite.

2. I copied the record of the Jaredites onto the gold plates.

3. I saw the destruction of many people.

4. I wrote instructions on the Sacrament prayers
    on the gold plates.

5. I was the last to handle the gold plates.

6. I am often referred to as an angel.

7. My father's name was Mormon.

Answer: My name is MORONI

1. I became King 463 years after Lehi left Jerusalem.

2. I translated the Jaredite record.

3. I was the last Nephite king before I counseled the people
    to elect judges instead.

4. I had four sons who were wicked but repented.

5. My father's name was Benjamin.

6. I lived in the city of Zarahemla.

7. I gave Alma authority to preside over the church.

Answer: My name is MOSIAH

1.   I had great faith.

2.   I lived at the time of the Tower of Babel.

3.   I saw that the Lord has a body shaped like our bodies.

4.   The Lord commanded my brother and me to build barges.

5.   My family's language was not confused when others were.

6.   I brought 16 stones for the Lord to touch so they would light up.

7.   My brother's name was Jared.

Answer: I am the brother of Jared—MAHONRI MORIANCUMER

1.   I left my country to go to the promised land.

2.   I made a covenant with the Lord.

3.   I had many, many descendants.

4.   I was a very wealthy man.

5.   My wife's name was changed from Sarai to Sarah.

6.   I received the priesthood from Melchizedek.

7.   One of my sons' name was Isaac.

Answer: My name is ABRAHAM

1.   I made a tent where I talked with Jehovah.

2.   I grew up in Egypt.

3.   My Father-in-law was Jethro.

4.   I never made it to the promised land.

5.   During my time the Feast of the Passover was instituted.

6. I called plagues down on Egypt.

7. I was given the ten commandments.

Answer: My name is MOSES

1. I was taken to Babylon as a young man.

2. I could interpret dreams and visions.

3. I prayed three times a day towards Jerusalem.

4. While in Babylon I refused to eat food other than that approved in the Mosaic Law.

5. My friends were Shadrach, Meshach and Abednego.

6. I interpreted a dream for King Nebuchadnezzar.

7. I was thrown into a lion's den.

Answer: My name is DANIEL

1. My father's name was Amittai.

2. My name means "Dove."

3. I did not want to go on a mission.

4. I ran away to Tarshish.

5. I lived during the reign of King Jeroboam.

6. I was angry with the Lord because he forgave some wicked people in Nineveh.

7. I was swallowed by a big fish.

Answer: My name is JONAH

1. I was a very wealthy man.

2. It was important that I marry someone of my own lineage and faith.

3. My mother's name was Rebekah.

4. I had a twin brother.

5. I worked 14 years for permission to marry the girl I loved.

6. I had 12 sons.

7. My name was changed to Israel.

Answer: My name is JACOB

1. I was a Hebrew.

2. I prophesied many things about your day.

3. I lived 700-800 years before Christ.

4. I counseled Kings in their political decisions.

5. During my time, my country split into two Kingdoms.

6. My words appear in the Book of Mormon as well as the Bible.

7. Some say my words are difficult to understand.

Answer: My name is ISAIAH

11
GUESSTURES

Purpose:

To have fun guessing words or phrases you hear at church.

Planning Ahead:

Assign or arrange refreshments.

Preparation: (last minute)

Make sure you have a clock or watch with a second hand. Copy the words following onto slips of paper and stack them, face down.

Process:

Part A: Opening song: "When I Go to Church" (Children's Songbook, page 157); Opening prayer; Scripture: D&C 109:7.

Part B: Divide the family into two teams. A representative from the first team goes to the front where he is given three paper slips turned face down. On a given signal he turns over the first one. He is given a few seconds to decide how he will act out the word and then, on another signal, he acts out the word for his team to guess. The timer calls out "move on" after 20 seconds. If his team hasn't guessed the word he must move on to the next. If they guess before the time is up he moves on and has the remaining time plus another ten seconds for the second word. He continues this way until he has tried for all three words given him. Each team gets a turn at sending up a member until all have had a turn, at which time the scores are totaled and a winning team declared. You may want to change the number of seconds allowed, depending on the knowledge, ages and quickness of your family members.

Part C: Refreshments; Closing prayer.

Guessture words and phrases

The iron rod	Amen	Latter-day Saints
Missionaries	Primary	Celestial Kingdom
Resurrection	Angel	The brass plates
Bishopric	Prayer	Search, Ponder and pray
Noah's ark	Brother	Choose the right
Revelation	Sacrifice	Study the scriptures
Sacred Grove	Temple	Sacrament bread
Plan of Salvation	Scouts	General Conference
Millennium	Eternity	Families are forever
Sunday School	Prophet	The ten commandments
High Council	Fasting	Redeem the dead
Adam and Eve	Journal	Celestial marriage
City of Enoch	Pioneers	Articles of Faith
Pre mortal life	Liahona	Garden of Eden
Family History	Baptism	Homemaking meeting
Home teachers	Hymns	Testimony meeting
Relief Society	Service	Plural marriage

12
CAMP OUT

Purpose:

To have fun together.

Planning Ahead:

Make sure there are sleeping bags or bedding for each member of the family.

Preparation: (last minute)

Announce that everyone is to meet at dusk for Family Home Evening.

Process:

Part A: Explain that tonight FHE will be a little different. You will start with refreshments.

Part B: Have everyone dress appropriately, gather up sleeping bags and go outside at dusk to sleep under the stars, perhaps on the trampoline or in a tent.

Opening song: "My Heavenly Father Loves Me" (Children's Songbook, page 228); Opening prayer, Scripture: D&C 104:14.

Part C:

Activity 1: Make up a story. Have one family member begin it and then each person picks up the story where the last left off. Some suggested beginnings: It was a cold, dark and stormy night . . . .

There it was . . . . Suzy (family member) had never seen anything like it before . . . .

One summer day we noticed a new family moving in next door. Little did we know . . . .

I came home from school one day to find . . . .

Mom was so excited, she couldn't wait to tell someone . . . .

Johnny (family member) was out on a bike ride when . . . .

Activity 2: Take turns telling jokes.

Activity 3: Try to find the "Big Dipper" or "Little Bear" in the Milky Way. Talk about Heavenly Father's creations.

Activity 4: Share testimonies.

Have prayer together before going to sleep.

13
PERSONAL HISTORIES

Purpose:

To begin keeping personal histories.

Planning Ahead:

Make sure you have a tape recorder and blank tapes. Assign or arrange for refreshments. Photocopy the Memory Teasers topics.

Preparation: (last minute)

Cut up the Photo-copied memory teasers and place them in a bowl or jar.

Process:

Part A: Opening song: "Families Can Be Together Forever" (Children's Songbook, page 188); Opening prayer; Scripture: 1 Nephi 1:1-3.

Part B: Have family members take turns pulling out slips of paper and answering the question on tape. Stop this activity before the children become bored with it.

Part C: Refreshments; Closing prayer.

Memory Teasers

What was your favorite animal or pet?

Describe the most serious illness you have had.

What do you want to be when you grow up?

Tell about your favorite aunt or uncle.

What is/was your childhood bedroom like?

What is/was your favorite book as a child, youth, and adult?

How does/did being the oldest, youngest, or middle child affect you?

Do you have a favorite General Authority? Who and why?

What do you feel has been the most significant world event in your lifetime?

What is your favorite food or meal?

Describe a Christmas of your childhood.

Describe the houses you have lived in. Do you still remember the addresses?

Describe a memorable Valentines day.

Tell about how, where, and when you learned to drive.

Tell about your first job.

What chores do/did you have when you were growing up?

Who is/was your best friend as a child? What do/did you like to do together?

Tell about your first date.

Describe a typical day of high school.

Have you ever gone on a blind date?

Do you have any heirlooms? How did you acquire them?

Who is/was your favorite teacher?

What are some of your favorite skills?

What is/was your favorite place to go with your family?

What is/was your favorite Television show as a child?

Where do you like to eat out at? What do you order?

What is the most exciting thing you ever did?

How does/did your mother spend her time?

Share a family tradition.

Tell about a favorite game you play or played when you were young.

What convinced you to marry your spouse?

What are you frightened of?

Tell about some of your neighbors as you grew up.

What did you do as a child that got you into the most trouble?

Describe a childhood birthday or Christmas present you remember.

Describe a typical day in your elementary school.

14
LETTERS TO THE FIELD

Purpose:

To show support for the missionaries serving from your ward.

Planning Ahead:

Assign or arrange for refreshments.

Preparation: (last minute)

Make sure you have a sheet of stationery or other paper for each missionary letter and a pen or pencil for each family member.

Process:

Part A: Opening song: "Called To Serve" (Children's Songbook, page 174); Opening prayer; Scripture: D&C 4:2-3.

Part B: Give each family member a piece of stationery or paper. Have them start a letter to one of the missionaries. (The youngest may need scribes). After writing a paragraph or two, each member will pass the paper on to another who will add his message, then again pass it on. Each letter circulates until all family members have written on it. This way several letters can be completed at the same time.

Part C: Refreshments; Closing prayer.

15
A WALK
IN THE WILDERNESS

Purpose:

To demonstrate that we all can find ourselves in situations where it is difficult to have a good attitude. Even though what is required of us may cause us to murmur, we also can find many things to be happy about. Only we can choose whether we will follow, and what our attitude will be when our leaders ask us to do something. Do not reveal the purpose of this activity until it is over.

Planning Ahead:

Purchase a sack of hard candy.

Preparation: (last minute)

Collect some small pebbles and have a Book of Mormon on hand.

Process:

Part A: Opening song: "Hum Your Favorite Song" (Children's Songbook, page 152); Opening prayer; Scripture: Ephesians 5:20.

Part B: Explain to the family that you are going for a walk. Give each one a piece of candy to put in his mouth (for sustenance) and a pebble to put in his shoe. Set an objective—something like going around the block and back in ten minutes, or walking by twenty houses before returning home. Choose something simple. Set up some rules: the family must stay together throughout the walk. They must walk, not run. If they make it back in the prescribed time there will be a reward.

Take the family on their "walk in the wilderness." During the walk you may notice some complaining about the pebble, but little or nothing said about the candy. Don't make a big deal about their complaints. Upon returning, ask the family what they noticed about the walk.

Explain that each of them had something to complain about, but they also had something to enjoy. What did they focus on? Liken this to the different attitudes of those who went with Lehi into the wilderness. Compare it to our attitudes when we are asked to do something by our parents or leaders. Read the story of the journey of Lehi and his family into the wilderness in 1 Nephi chapter 2. (For extended reading, you may read 1 Nephi chapters 1-5 and 7.) Liken the family members' attitudes to those who went with Lehi into the wilderness. Compare it to our attitudes when we are asked to do something by our parents or leaders.

Part C: Refreshments (the reward); Closing prayer.

16
FLOUR FUN

Purpose:

To reinforce the principle of repentance. As a person "cuts" into his life with sin, things will eventually come crashing down around him. After making a mistake it can be messy to clean up.

Planning Ahead:

Assign or arrange for refreshments.

Preparation: (last minute)

You will need a plate, a butter knife, a cup or glass, a dime and some flour.

Process:

Part A: Opening song: "Listen, Listen" (Children's Songbook, page 107)); Opening prayer; Scripture: Matthew 26:41.

Part B: Read the story of Alma in Mosiah chapter 27.

Fill the glass with flour. Place the plate over the cup, hold them together firmly, and turn them both over. Carefully lift the glass off the flour—the hill of flour will be left standing on the plate. Gently place the dime on top of the flour mound.

Each player than takes a turn slicing off some flour from the flour mound with the knife, taking care not to cut too close to the dime.

They continue taking turns until one player makes the dime fall. That person must then search for and retrieve the dime using only his lips and teeth. Everyone will probably want to play this several times.

When the game is over, compare the game with sin. If we get too close to temptation and do not remove ourselves, we are in danger. There is some excitement in seeing how close we can come, but that is what Satan does to entice us. Even if we are able to retrieve the dime, there is still a mess. Likewise, even after we repent, there are often consequences which are difficult or even impossible to remove. Ask for some examples like: If you steal something, even if you return it, people may not trust you again. If you are immoral you may repent, but you still may have to live with a sexually transmitted disease.

Part C: Refreshments; Closing prayer.

17
CLAY NATIVITY

Purpose:

To explore your family's artistic side.

Planning Ahead:

Arrange for or assign refreshments. Make sure you have flour, salt, and acrylic paints in assorted colors (craft stores usually have these in primary color combinations at a reasonable price), paint brushes, and an acrylic finishing spray.

You may decide to make the nativity scene one week and paint it another. This buys some time to pick up the paints and spray you need. You may choose to leave your nativity scene unpainted.

Preparation: (last minute)

Follow the recipe to make clay:

> 2 cups Flour
> 1 cup Salt
> 3/4 cup hot water

Place hot water and salt in a bowl and let it dissolve for 5 minutes. Add the flour and knead it until it is soft but not sticky. You need not do this ahead but may choose to make the dough as part of your activity.

Process:

Part A: Opening song: "Mary's Lullaby" (Children's Songbook, page 44); Opening prayer; Scripture: Luke 2:6, 7.

Part B: Shape the clay as desired into Baby Jesus, Mary, Joseph, Shepherds, Wise men, Lambs, Cows, Angel. Be creative! Use toothpicks and other utensils to shape and contour. A garlic press could be used to make hair and wool. Use a little water to stick parts together, or use glue when they have cooled.

Place dough shapes on a foil covered cookie sheet. Bake at 250 degrees for about 2 hours. Check periodically. Remove them from the oven and cool. Paint as desired. When dry, spray with clear acrylic spray. Let your creativity flow!

Prepare a special place to display your homemade nativity scene.

Part C: Refreshments; Closing prayer.

18
SCRIPTURE COOKIES

Purpose:

To become better acquainted with the books in the standard works.

Planning Ahead:

Have on hand the following ingredients: butter, milk, sugar (sweet cane), eggs, flour, cinnamon, salt, baking soda (leaven), oats, raisins.

Preparation: (last minute)

Gather copies of the standard works.

Process:

Part A: Opening song: "Search, Ponder and Pray" (Children's Songbook, page 109); Opening prayer; Scripture: 2 Nephi 4:15.

Part B: Read the scriptures one by one, decide what the ingredient is, and have the children prepare the correct amount.

Follow the recipe to mix and bake the cookies.

Part C: Cookies for refreshments; Closing prayer.

Scripture Cookie Recipe

3/4 cup   "The words of his mouth were smoother than _____"
(Psalm 55:21)

1/3 cup   "Come unto me all ye ends of the earth, buy _____
and honey" (2 Nephi 26:25)

1½ cups   "to what purpose cometh there to me . . . the_____
from a far country?" (Jeremiah 6:20)

2   "As one gathereth _____that are left, have I gathered all the earth" (Isaiah 10:14)

2 cups   "And Solomon's provision for one day was thirty measures of fine_____" (1 Kings 4:22)

1 tsp.   "take thou also unto thee principle spices, . . . and of
sweet _____ half so much" (Exodus 30:23)

1 tsp.   "ye are the _____ of the earth" (Matthew 5:13)

1/2 tsp.   "Know ye not that a little_____leaveneth the whole
lump?" (1 Corinthians 5:6)

3 cups   "Nevertheless, . . . _____ for the horse" (Doctrine
and Covenants 89:17)

1 cup   "And they gave him . . . two clusters of _____"
(1 Samuel 30:12)

1. Beat the first four ingredients together.
2. Mix in the remaining ingredients.
3. Drop by teaspoonfuls onto a greased cookie sheet.
4. Bake at 350 degrees F (175 degrees C) for 15 minutes.

19
FAMILY OLYMPICS

Purpose:

To enjoy a fun evening of friendly Olympic competition with some other families.

Planning Ahead:

Invite two or more other families to your Family Olympics. Give some notice if possible, but don't be afraid to call somebody at the last minute. Assign or arrange for refreshments. Prepare the awards (something simple like ribbons homemade from wrapping paper or even brown paper sacks, canning lids painted with a number 1, or even candy bars)

Preparation: (last minute)

Choose the games for competition and collect assorted items for those games. (See the individual games following.) When the other families have arrived, choose a couple of referees to keep the events moving and make all final decisions.

Process:

Part A: Opening song: "Do As I'm Doing" (Children's Songbook, page 276); Opening Prayer; Scripture: D&C 121:9.

Part B: Give each family a piece of paper and crayons or markers. Have them design a family flag and choose a family song (keep them short), to be sung each time they win an event. Then proceed through each event. Give out awards at the end of each event. Have every one sing the winning family's chosen song.

Part C: Refreshments; Closing prayer.

Olympic Events

FOUR-LAP RELAY

A relay where each lap is something different. (cartwheels, running, walking backwards, wheelbarrow, etc.) The first team to finish the last lap wins. You could either choose four people or let everyone do it and even it up by smaller families having members go more than once.

MOM-CALLING CONTEST

Line Moms up side by side across an open area and blindfold them. Line up the children on the other side, a fairly good distance apart, with siblings grouped together. At the signal, the kids all start calling for their mothers.

The first Mom to find her kids and walk over to them blindfolded is the winner.

HOUSE of CARDS

Give each family a deck of cards and 10 minutes to build a house of cards as high as they can. The family with the highest, most elaborate house, when the bell rings, is the winner.

PENNY-TOSSING CONTEST

Each player holds five pennies. Players take turns throwing the pennies, one at a time, in three bowls at various distances from them. The farthest bowl is worth 3 points, the middle bowl 2 points, and the closest bowl 1 point. The family with the most points at the end is the winner.

KNOCK DOWN THE CANS

This game could be used to see which Dad can knock down the cans. Pile 6 cans in a pyramid. (If the cans are full, use a real baseball, but if they are empty use a rolled up pad of socks.) Everyone has two chances to knock down all of the cans. The one with the most knocked-over cans is the winner.

These are just a few ideas; the possibilities are endless. Obstacle courses, ball throwing, three-legged races, pie eating, stick pulling, etc. Be imaginative, and have a ball!

20
TIC-TAC-TOE

Purpose:

A fun review of your family's scripture knowledge.

Planning Ahead:

Buy two different kinds of candy. (e.g. M & M's and Starbursts, or Skittles and midget Tootsie Rolls).

Preparation: (last minute)

You will need a big piece of paper or a dry erase board with a Tic-Tac-Toe frame drawn on it. Questions for the competition are found on pages 80-94 at the back of the book.

Process:

Part A: Opening song: "Seek the Lord Early" (Children's Songbook, page 108); Opening Prayer; Scripture: John 5:39.

Part B: Explain that you are going to play Tic-Tac-Toe, but instead of just getting the square for free you have to earn it by answering a gospel question correctly.

Divide into two teams. Give each team one kind of candy. If the team answers correctly, they get to put a piece of candy on the square. If the answer is incorrect, the other team gets a chance to answer correctly and to put a piece of candy on the square. If both teams answer incorrectly, the square remains blank. The first team to get Tic-Tac-Toe is the winner and gets all the candy on the board.

This should go into a bowl for their team to share. Keep playing until the candy or the questions run out.

Part C: Eat the candy (you may want to add something else); Closing prayer.

21
DINNER FOR A DOLLAR

Purpose:

To have a fun family outing shopping for bargains and fun.

Planning Ahead:

Make sure you have a one-dollar bill for each member of the family. It would be fun to invite another family to participate in this activity.

Preparation: (last minute)

none.

Process:

Part A: Opening song: "Quickly I'll Obey" (Children's Songbook, page 197); Opening prayer; Scripture: Colossians 3:20.

Part B: Gather the family together. Explain that for dinner tonight everyone will be given a dollar to go to the store and buy something they would like to have for dinner that evening. Explain that the food will be pooled, and all family members will get to partake of whatever they choose. They can work together with someone, or by themselves—it is up to them. This fun activity will open up opportunities for discussions during dinner on such topics as making good choices, the consequences of our choices, what our family's likes and dislikes are, the importance of good planning, and setting goals.

Part C: Closing prayer.

22
LIGHTS OUT

Purpose:

To become aware of what might be needed in case of a power failure.

Planning Ahead:

Call home and let Mom in on the fun. Perhaps she could put off starting dinner. You may want to have a snack or back-up dinner in mind for later in the evening.

Preparation: (last minute)

none.

Process:

Part A: Dad turns off the power upon arriving home. Suddenly there will be no television, no video games, no lights, no furnace, no microwave. You get the picture! Dad and Mom should play along as if it is a surprise to them as well.

Part B: Call everyone together and have prayer. Assign someone to locate some source of light and then let the evening progress as normally as possible—dinner, homework, entertainment. Don't solve anyone's problems—let the children figure out "plan B" for themselves.

Part C: After some time has elapsed (perhaps and hour or two), call everyone together while still in the dark and ask a few questions.

Possible Questions

What were our immediate needs?

What did we wish we had the most?

What things could we not do without?

What if this lasted for days?

What if Mom and Dad were not home?

If this happened to the entire neighborhood, would we be able to help others?

If this lasted a long time and we had food and heat, what would we do to entertain ourselves?

Turn the power back on and formulate a written preparation plan. Decide how to implement it.

Have refreshments (or dinner if necessary). Closing prayer.

23
SMILES
ACROSS THE MILES

Purpose:

To encourage the family to celebrate day-to-day experiences with loved ones far away. In particular, a birthday party for Grandma, Grandpa or a missionary.

Planning Ahead:

You will need a video camera and new tape. (If you don't own one, perhaps you can borrow one for the occasion.) Plan for a cake, and perhaps some presents to be boxed and sent later. Don't forget, no self respecting birthday party is complete without party games so plan for some. You will also need a piece of paper and pencil for each family member.

Preparation: (last minute)

Send everyone throughout the house in search of decorations for one room where the party will be held. You will be surprised at the decorating goodies to be found around the house. Balloons, crepe paper, toilet paper, ribbon, hair ribbons, foil, flowers from the yard, stuffed animals to name a few. Decorate the room for the party.

Process:

Part A: Opening song: "Love One Another" (Children's Songbook, page 136); Opening prayer; Scripture: John 13:34-35.

Pass out paper and pencils. Have each person write something they love about "Grandma." Put these in a basket for later.

Part B: Let the party begin! With the camera rolling, everyone travels to the decorated room, leading Grandma (the camera man). Once there, yell Surprise!

Happy Birthday! Sing Happy Birthday to her. She'll feel as though she is right in the room with you. Take her around the room, filming the decorations, cake and presents. At some point, blow out the candles and play some games. At the end of the party, have each person draw a piece of paper out of the basket and read what was written to Grandma.

Everyone then can have a chance to tell her how they love and miss her. At the end of the evening, box up the presents with some of the decorations, ready to be mailed. This will be a once-in-a-life-time treasure.

Part C: Cut and serve the cake. Closing prayer

Suggested Games

1. Have the kids draw a festive flower on paper. Cut out the center and play "Pin the Center on the Flower" (a person is blindfolded and tries to attach the center to the middle of the flower).

2. Fill a bag with mini-marshmallows, chocolate chips, cereal or small candies (whatever you have on hand). Players sit in a circle and pass the bag, while Dad whistles or sings a song (a tape can be used if you are really prepared). When the music stops the person holding the

bag gets something out of the bag. The game continues until the treats are gone.

3. Put cotton balls in a bowl. Blindfold someone and hand them a spatula. Dump the balls onto the floor. The fun begins when the person tries to scoop up the cotton balls.

4. Beans and Straws: Put some dried beans on 2 separate chairs. Divide into two teams. Each team member gets a straw. On the command, each team races to their designated chair and sucks a bean to the straw. The winning team is the one that returns with the beans the fastest.

24
FAMILY TIME CAPSULE

Purpose:

A fun way to preserve some memories and capture the growth of the family through the years.

Planning Ahead:

Assign or arrange for refreshments. Find a clean tin can, box, ice cream bucket or any other suitable container to use as the capsule. Prepare enough questionnaires for each family member. As an option plan for a tape or video recorder and blank audio or video tape.

Preparation: (last minute)

none.

Process:

Part A: Opening song: "Here We Are Together" (Children's Songbook, page 261); Opening prayer, Scripture: Moses 6:46.

Part B: Explain to the family that a time capsule contains items that tell about the people who buried it and the time in which they lived. Explain that it will be opened at a later date and let your family choose the date. Also decide on a location in which to hide or "bury" your time capsule.

Ask each person to select one or more "treasures" to represent him or her. It need not be a real treasure. A favorite comic, hair tie, small toy or whatever they wish. Perhaps a school photo of each or a family photo could be included. If you have a tape recorder, you could include a tape of everyone's voices. Have each family member fill out the questionnaire. Fill the container with the papers and objects. Seal the container and label it with the day's date and your family's name, as well as the date you plan to open it.

"Bury" the time capsule by storing it somewhere where it will be easily found in three, five or ten years.

Part C: Refreshments; Closing prayer

QUESTIONNAIRE

Name_____   Date _____

Nickname_____   Date of Birth _____

Favorites:

Food_____   Movie _____

Book_____   Friend _____

TV Show_____   Song _____

Article of clothing _____

Holiday and Why _____

_____

About Me:

Thing I like best about my family _____

Thing I would like to change about me _____

What I want to be doing in 5 years _____

How old I will be when I am very old _____

What I think about Heavenly Father _____

_____

What I am most thankful for _____

Some things I am good at _____

_____

My family responsibilities are_____

_____

On the back of the paper make a tracing of your hand and foot print.

25
WHO SAID IT?

Purpose:

To become acquainted with the unique character and contributions of the past and present presidents of the Church.

Planning ahead:

You might like to obtain pictures of the Church presidents from your ward library. This is not necessary for the activity. Arrange for refreshments.

Preparation: (last minute)

Make strips of paper with the names of the presidents. Each must be on a separate sheet. Make two copies—one for each team. The names, in order, are:

1. Joseph Smith Jr.
2. Brigham Young
3. John Taylor
4. Wilford Woodruff
5. Lorenzo Snow
6. Joseph F. Smith
7. Heber J. Grant
8. George Albert Smith
9. David O. McKay
10. Joseph Fielding Smith
11. Harold B. Lee
12. Spencer W. Kimball
13. Ezra Taft Benson
14. Howard W. Hunter
15. Gordon B. Hinckley

Process:

Part A: Opening hymn: "We Thank Thee O God For A Prophet" (Hymns, page 19); Opening prayer; Scripture: Luke 1:70.

Part B:

Activity 1 - Send the children to find the following: some paper or tin foil wadded into a ball, and a glass or paper cup. Also, something to be used as a golf stick-like a cardboard tube from wrapping paper or a yard stick. Divide into two teams. Hand each team a set of the Presidents' names (in jumbled order). Set a timer for a minute, or count slowly to sixty. Each team must put the names in order as quickly as possible. This is a learning exercise as well as a race, so repeat the competition several times.

Activity 2 - Time to play Putt Putt. Each team works together and all members can contribute. Give a time limit for an answer. If team A cannot answer, team B gets a chance. Set up three lines of masking tape at different distances from the putting hole (cup). If a team identifies the quote correctly, they get to putt from the closest line. If they need one extra clue, they putt from the second line, and if they need the final clue they put from the furthest line. They score 1, 2 or 3 points accordingly. The highest-scoring team wins!

Part C: Refreshments; Closing prayer.

Quotes For The Putt Putt Game

"Happiness is the object and design of our existence; and will be the end thereof, if we pursue the path that leads to it; and this path is virtue, uprightness, faithfulness, holiness and keeping all the commandments of God."

—Joseph Smith Jr.

"It matters not whether you or I feel like praying; when it comes time to pray, pray. If you do not feel like it, we should pray till we do."

—Brigham Young

"I felt that the Lord had preserved me by a special act of mercy; that my time had not yet come, and that I still had a work to preform upon the earth."

—John Taylor

"I feel to exhort and to counsel you my young friends, to listen to the voice of God and obey it while you are young."

—Wilford Woodruff

"As man now is, God once was; As God now is, man may become."

—Lorenzo Snow

"If the saints obey this counsel [to hold Family Home Evening], we promise that great blessings will result. Love at home and obedience to parents will increase."

—Joseph F. Smith

"Keep the commandments of God. That is my keynote speech, just those few words; keep the commandments of God."

—Heber J. Grant

"I would be a friend to the friendless and find joy in ministering to the needs of the poor . . . I would not be an enemy to any living soul."

—George Albert Smith

"Every member a missionary."

—David O. McKay

"There are no cures for the ills of the world except the gospel of Jesus Christ . . . the Lord loves you and wants you to receive the full blessings of the gospel."

—Joseph Fielding Smith

"The greatest miracles I see today are not necessarily the healing of sick bodies, but the greatest miracles I see are the healing of sick souls; we are reaching out to the sick, because they are precious in the sight of the Lord, and we want no-one to feel forgotten."

—Harold B. Lee

"Do it." or, "We do not go to Sabbath meetings to be entertained or even solely to be instructed. We go to worship the Lord."

—Spencer W. Kimball

"There is a power in the book that will begin to flow into your lives the moment you begin to seriously study the book."

—Ezra Taft Benson

"I invite all members of the church to live with ever more attention to the life and example of the Lord Jesus Christ, especially the love and hope and compassion he displayed. I pray that we will treat each other with more kindness, more patience, more courtesy and for-giveness."

—Howard W. Hunter

"We have nothing to fear. God is at the helm. He will overrule for the good of the work. He will shower down blessings upon those who walk in obedience to his commandments."

—Gordon B. Hinckley

ADDITIONAL CLUES

1. He had an operation on his leg without anesthesia.
   He was named after his father.

2. He is known for his organizational skills.
   He led the pioneers to Utah.

3. He was with the Prophet during the martyrdom.
   He served as President of the Church between 1880 and 1887.

4. He had many accidents when he was a child.
   During his presidency, Fast Day was changed from Thursday
   to the first Sunday of each month.

5. He taught the importance of tithing.
   He had a "snow-white" beard.

6. He healed a little blind boy in Holland.
   His father was Hyrum Smith.

7. His father died when he was nine days old.
   He organized the Church Welfare Program.

8. He shipped food and clothes to Europe after World War II.
   He was the first Church president to appear on television
   in General Conference.

9. His motto was "What'er thou art, act well thy part."
   He served as President of the Church for 19 years.

10. He served for 69 years in the Church Historian's Office.
    He was the tenth President of the Church.

11. He saw to it that thousands of families were provided
    for at Christmas.
    He served as the president of the Church for only 17 months.

12. He had a great love for the Lamanite people.
    His voice was easily recognized because he spoke in a whisper
    after throat surgery.

13. At one time he was the U.S. Secretary of Agriculture.
    As the prophet, he stressed the importance of studying
    the Book of Mormon.

14. As a young man, he played in a dance band.
    As the Prophet, he stressed the importance of
    attending the temple.

15. He was known for the building of many temples.
    He traveled throughout the world more than any other Prophet.

26
NAME GAME

Purpose:

To build a comfortable recognition of the books in the scriptures.

Planning Ahead:

Assign or arrange for refreshments.
Prepare two sets of the book names so there can be a competition.

Preparation: (last minute)

You will need a piece of paper and a pencil or a white erase board.
Decide on which book of scriptures you will study.

Process:

Part A: Opening song: "The Books in the New Testament" (Children's Songbook, page 116); Opening prayer; Scripture: 2 Nephi 4:15.

Part B: If the family is large enough, divide into two teams. If not, the family can race the clock. To introduce the subject you will be studying, write on the paper or board spaces to correspond to the letters in the particular book of scripture.

For example, ___ _____ for the New Testament

Hand each team a set of names of books from the New Testament as well as a copy of the New Testament. See who can put the books in the correct order the fastest. Do this as many time as the children enjoy it. You will notice it becomes much easier and faster. See if you can beat your own times. The family members may notice, for instance, that there are four books of John in the New Testament. This can be used in a follow-up discussion.

Another game is to name the first book and see if the person next to you can name the next in order. Continue around the family. Each time you can go no further, begin again and see if you can go further the next time.

Part C: Refreshments; Closing prayer.

BOOKS OF THE NEW TESTAMENT

Matthew	1 Timothy
Mark	2 Timothy
Luke	Titus
John	Philemon
The Acts	To The Hebrews
The Epistle to the Romans	The Epistle of James
1 Corinthians	1 Peter
2 Corinthians	2 Peter
Galatians	1 John
Ephesians	2 John
Philippians	3 John
Colossians	Jude
1 Thessalonians	Revelation
2 Thessalonians	

BOOKS OF THE OLD TESTAMENT

Genesis	2 Chronicles	Daniel
Exodus	Ezra	Hosea
Leviticus	Nehemiah	Joel
Numbers	Esther	Amos
Deuteronomy	Job	Obadiah
Joshua	Psalms	Jonah
Judges	Proverbs	Micah
Ruth	Ecclesiastes	Nahum
1 Samuel	The Song of Solomon	Habakkuk
2 Samuel	Isaiah	Zephaniah
1 Kings	Jeremiah	Haggai
2 Kings	Lamentations	Zechariah
1 Chronicles	Ezekiel	Malachi

BOOKS OF THE BOOK OF MORMON

1 Nephi	Omni	Third Nephi
2 Nephi	The Words of Mormon	Fourth Nephi
Jacob	Mosiah	Mormon
Enos	Alma	Ether
Jarom	Helaman	Moroni

BOOKS OF THE PEARL OF GREAT PRICE

Moses	Joseph Smith—Matthew
Abraham	Joseph Smith—History
	The Articles of Faith

27
BLANKET THE WORLD

Purpose:

To appreciate and share the value of the Book of Mormon with others.

Planning Ahead:

You will need a new copy of the Book of Mormon for each family member, to be given away. Arrange for refreshments. Perhaps some "Ammonade" (lemonade) and frozen "Neefries" (french fries).

Preparation: (last minute)

Gather together a roll of toilet paper and 2 blankets.

Process:

Part A: Opening song: "Book Of Mormon Stories" (Children's Songbook, page 118); Opening prayer; Scripture: D&C 18:15.

Part B:

Activity 1- Pass around a roll of toilet paper and each family member must take as many squares as he "needs." Give no further explanation. When everyone is sufficiently "covered," explain that for each square of toilet paper a person has, he must tell a favorite Book of Mormon story. No stories may be repeated. If squares are left, the assignment is to report back with a story at the next Family Home Evening.

Activity 2 - Divide the family into two teams. Give each a blanket. Explain that the blanket represents the Book of Mormon and the living room floor represents the world. The object is for each team to run to a clear space (the world) and cover it with the blanket (blanket it with the book of Mormon). Then each team member must get on his/her blanket and try to turn the blanket over without anyone falling off.

If someone falls off, they must replace the blanket and start again. See which team turns the blanket over first.

Activity 3 - Give everyone in the family a new Book of Mormon, a piece of paper, and a pen. Explain that each family member will write his testimony on the paper. Then the testimonies will be typed on the computer and run off, so they can be glued into the various copies of the Book of Mormon, in the front of the book. Invite someone to say a special prayer to invite the Spirit and ask for inspiration. Have each one sign and date his testimony.

Make plans to invite the missionaries over for dinner to present them with the books, or plan to mail them to missionaries serving from your ward.

Activity 4 - Take the opportunity for Mom and Dad to bear their testimonies of the Book of Mormon. Others may wish to bear their testimonies also.

Part C: Refreshments; Closing prayer.

28
JUST CALL ME DAVID

Purpose:

To teach that many of us are "joiners." We already have a great cause to join. Let's be like David and defeat our own Goliaths.

Planning Ahead:

You need a roll of butcher paper 10 feet long, or sheets of copy paper taped end to end to make 10 feet; some tape; and tin foil. You also need 2 ten-pound sacks and 1 five-pound sack of sugar. (Raid your food-storage shelves.)

Arrange for refreshments—perhaps "Goliath" giant cookies.

Preparation: (last minute)

none.

Process:

Part a: Opening hymn: "Who's on the Lord's Side Who?" (Hymns, page 175); Opening prayer; Scripture: 1 Samuel 17:37.

Part B: Read together, taking turns, the story of David and Goliath in 1 Samuel chapter 17.

After the story is told, start running the 10-foot length of paper up the wall and ask, "How tall do you think Goliath really was?" Have the children tell you when to stop. Roll the paper up the wall and onto the ceiling if necessary. Ask the family how they would like to face some-one this size who was very mean. Ask the family to guess how heavy the spearhead was on Goliath's spear. Start to load the sugar into someone's arms. Explain that it was 26 lbs. Ask if they know how much his armor weighed and after some guessing explain that it weighed as much as 2, 3 or 4 children—150 lbs.

Ask some questions about David.

Why did he think he might be able to defeat someone like Goliath? Was he afraid?

Was he prepared with a skill?

Talk about the things in our lives that we struggle to overcome today. As they are suggested, list them on the paper Goliath. For example:

hitting	cheating on papers
swearing	disobedience to parents
stealing	losing our tempers
smoking	rudeness
pride	being mean
gossip	self-pity
laziness	inactivity
lying	discouragement
drinking	belittling or making fun of others

After a sufficient number are up there, play the following game:

Roll pieces of tin foil into "stones." Take turns aiming at "Goliath" and defeating a weakness. Of course, older children must stand fur-ther away from "Goliath" than younger children. As someone hits a weakness, discuss ways of overcoming that particular problem. Perhaps older family members can look the word up in the index or topical guide to the Scriptures for added insight.

Part C: Refreshments; Closing prayer.

29
WHAT'S ON YOUR MIND?

Purpose:

To illustrate the importance of putting good things in our minds so the world does not fill it for us.

Planning Ahead:

Arrange for refreshments.

Preparation: (last minute)

none.

Process:

Part A: Opening song; "The Wise Man and the Foolish Man" (Children's Songbook, page 281); Opening prayer; Scripture: Matthew 7:24-27.

Part B: Divide the family into teams, or play as individuals. Read a phrase from the Commercials List, following. See if the children can identify the products. Have the children come up with some of their own to test each other. Point out how easily our minds fill up with information when we are exposed to it repeatedly. Explain that if we do not actively fill our minds with good books, scriptures, good movies and games, then other things which may not be so pleasant or good will take their place.

Now suggest filling your minds with something good, in one of the most successful ways the commercials do—by setting something to music. Make sure everyone is familiar with the tune of "The Wheels on the Bus Go Round and Round" and replace the words with the words of Alma 5:14-15, as follows:

The Wheels on the bus go round and round
And now behold I ask of you

Round and round - round and round
My brethren - of the church

The wheels on the bus go round and round
Have ye spiritually been born of God

All . . . through the town
Have ye received His image in your countenance

Experiment with some other scriptures set to music. Sometimes adjusting the words to the music can be tricky but fun. For example:

Mosiah 2:17 to the tune of "Happy Birthday to You"

Happy birthday to you
Behold I tell you these things

Happy birthday to you
That ye may learn wisdom

Happy birthday dear Suzy
That ye may learn that when ye are in the service
   of your fellow beings

Happy birthday to you
Ye are only in the service of your God

Try D&C 88:119 to the tune of "Here We Are Together"

Here we are together
Organize yourselves pre

Together together
pare every needful thing

Oh here we are together
And establish a house

In our family
a house of prayer

There's Suzy and Billy
a house of fasting

And Mary and Johnny
a house of faith

Oh here we are together
A House of learning

Together, together
a house of glory

Oh here we are together in our family
a house of order a house of God

Part C: Refreshments; Closing prayer.

Commercial Slogans

It's an up thing 7UP

Bet ya can't eat just one . . . . Lays potato chips

10 cents a minute . . . . Sprint or At&T

The headache medicine . . . . Exedrin

Pain killer most recommended by hospitals . . . . Tylenol

Just for the taste of it . . . . Diet Coke

No more tears . . . . Johnson's baby shampoo

Two all beef patties, special sauce, lettuce, cheese,
pickles, onions on a sesame seed bun . . . . McDonalds Big Mac

Just do it . . . . Nike

Obey your thirst . . . . Sprite

Yo quiero . . . . Taco Bell

Melt in your mouth, not in your hands . . . . M&M's

Um Um Good . . . . Campbell's Soup

Hair so healthy it shines . . . . Pantene

Like a rock . . . . Chevrolet trucks

It does a body good . . . . Milk

Give us a week, we'll take off the weight . . . . Slimfast

Better than potatoes . . . . Stovetop

30
SHADOW BLUFF

Purpose:

To have fun playing a variation on "Charades" to illustrate the point that appearances can be deceiving.

Planning Ahead:

You will need a blank wall or a tacked up sheet for a screen, a bright light that can cause a somewhat-focused beam.

Preparation: (last minute)

none.

Process:

Part A: Opening song: "Teach Me To Walk in the Light" (Children's Songbook, page 177); Opening prayer; Scripture: Ether 4:12.

Part B: The person who is 'IT' sits on the floor in the middle of the room facing the blank wall. The light is placed behind 'IT', shining on the wall, and all the lights are turned off. One by one, the other players pass behind 'IT' and in front of the light. Looking straight ahead at the shadow on the wall (you could fashion some kind of blinders, or make a tent out of blankets so they can not see behind them), 'IT' tries to call out the identity of the player crossing behind them. Players may disguise their shadows in any way to confuse 'IT'. The player whose identity is guessed correctly becomes 'IT'.

TIP- Don't let your height give you away. Moving closer or farther away from the light will make you appear taller or shorter. Things are not always what they seem. Have a discussion about appearances, involving things that are made to appear glamorous but are really not good for you—such as alcohol, cigarettes, and the trappings of the world. You could also have a discussion on not judging others by their appearances.

Part C: Refreshments; Closing prayer.

31
Quiz Questions

The following pages contain questions from each of the Standard Works to be used in the activities that involve quizzes. Note that they are divided into 3 levels of difficulty.

New Testament
(Answers are on page 83.)

EASY

1. In what town was Jesus born?

2. Did Jesus write any of the books in the New Testament?

3. What sign appeared in the sky at the birth of Jesus?

4. True or False: A woman of great faith was once healed by touching Jesus's clothes.

5. Who was the first man to be resurrected?

6. What was Peter's occupation?

7. One of Christ's apostles betrayed Him. Who was it?

8. True or False: John the Apostle and John the Baptist are the same person.

9. How many apostles did the Savior originally place in His church?

10. True or False: There were teachers and deacons, elders, seventies, and high priests in the Church in the days of the apostles.

11. Name the river in which Jesus was baptized.

12. Name the first book in the New Testament.

13. What were the names of Jesus's father and mother on earth?

14. True or False: John the Baptist and John the Revelator are the same person.

15. In what town did Jesus live while he was a boy?

AVERAGE

16. Will everyone be resurrected at the beginning of the Millennium?

17. True or False: Christ held the Melchizedek priesthood.

18. In what city was the Last Supper held?

19. Who is the author of the Epistles to the Corinthians?

20. Were any of Christ's apostles married?

21. Who were the three leaders of Jesus's apostles?

22. Who preached the Sermon on the Mount?

23. Name the four books known as the Gospels in the New Testament.

24. What was Saul's name changed to?

25. What apostle wrote the last book of the New Testament?

26. How did the apostles confer the Gift of the Holy Ghost?

27. What did the Lord give the apostles when He said," This is my body which is given for you; this do in remembrance of me"?

28. Has anyone else ever been resurrected besides the Savior?

29. Name five of the Epistles of Paul.

30. Which apostle was asked by Jesus to care for His mother?

HARD

31. What relative of Jairus did Jesus restore to life?

32. In which book of the New Testament is baptism for the dead mentioned?

33. Who said, "Saul, Saul, why persecutest thou me?"

34. What crime had the two men committed who were crucified with Jesus?

35. What king said, "Paul, almost thou persuadest me to be a Christian"?

36. To whom did Jesus say, "To day shalt thou be with me in paradise"?

37. To which Apostle did the resurrected Christ ask three times, "lovest thou me?"

38. How long did the black darkness last which spread over the face of the land at the crucifixion of Jesus?

39. What two prophets, besides Jesus, did the three Apostles see at the Transfiguration?

40. Who took Judas Iscariot's place among the Twelve?

41. Which two Apostles were called "Sons of Thunder"?

42. Name two sets of brothers who were among Christ's apostles.

43. Where did Jesus tell Peter he would find some money to pay taxes?

44. Which Apostle cut off the ear of Malchus, a member of the band who came to take Jesus captive?

45. Name the Garden where Jesus prayed just before He was betrayed.

New Testament Answers

EASY
1. Bethlehem
2. No
3. A Star
4. True
5. Jesus
6. A fisherman
7. Judas Iscariot
8. False
9. Twelve
10. True
11. Jordan
12. Matthew
13. Joseph and Mary
14. False
15. Nazareth

AVERAGE
16. No
17. True
18. Jerusalem
19. Paul
20. Yes

21. Peter, James and John
22. Jesus
23. Matthew, Mark, Luke, John
24. Paul
25. John
26. By the Laying on of Hands
27. Bread
28. Yes
29. Romans, 1 Corinthians, 2 Corinthians, Galatians, Ephesians, Philippians, Colossians, 1 Thessalonians, 1 Timothy, 2 Timothy, Titus, Philemon, Hebrews
30. John

HARD
31. His daughter
32. 1 Corinthians
33. Jesus
34. Robbery
35. Agrippa
36. Thief on the Cross
37. Peter
38. Three hours
39. Moses and Elijah
40. Matthias
41. James and John
42. James and John; Andrew and Simon Peter
43. In the mouth of a Fish
44. Peter
45. Gethsemane

OLD TESTAMENT
(Answers are on page 86.)

EASY

1. What was the name of the baby that was found by the Pharaoh's daughter?

2. Name the man who lost his strength when his hair was cut by his enemies.

3. Who was commanded by the Lord to build an ark to escape the flood?

4. Name the prophet of the Lord who was swallowed by a whale.

5. Who was the first woman to dwell on earth?

6. What Prophet led the children of Israel out of bondage by the Egyptians?

7. True or False: In Noah's time, before the flood, there were many languages spoken.

8. Who was Abel's mother?

9. Name the garden in which Adam and Eve lived.

10. What was Lot's wife changed into because she would not keep the commandment of God?

11. Name the second book in the Old Testament.

12. Who committed the first murder?

13. Who killed the giant Goliath?

14. What prophet did the Lord test by asking him to sacrfice his son, Isaac?

15. What did Noah see that made him know that land was near?

AVERAGE

16. What was the name of Moses' brother, who assisted him in leading the children of Israel to the promised land?

17. Which of Jacob's sons became a leader in Egypt and saved his family from famine?

18. Which book in the Old Testament is also called the First Book of Moses?

19. Who did Moses make his successor by the laying on of hands?

20. Who was taken to heaven in a chariot of fire?

21. What was the city whose walls came tumbling down at the loud shout of the Israelite armies?

22. What king of Israel is remembered for the beautiful temple he built?

23. Who was Jacob's twin brother?

24. What prophet wrote the longest book in the Old Testament?

25. Name three of the ten commandments given to Moses.

26. What is the last book in the Old Testament?

27. What was the name of the tower the people built to try and reach God?

28. On what mountain did Moses receive the Ten Commandments?

29. Who said "Choose you this day whom ye will serve; . . . but as for me and my house, we will serve the LORD"?

30. In the Old Testament, who's name was changed to Israel?

HARD

31. Name the other two sons of Noah besides Shem who were saved in the Ark.

32. Name the fifth book in the Old Testament.

33. Name the other companion of Shadrach and Meshach, who was saved with them from being burned to death.

34. For what King did Daniel interpret a dream about a stone rolling down a mountain?

35. Who was Ruth's mother-in-law?

36. Who was the man in whose fields Ruth gleaned?

37. Who succeeded Saul as King of Israel?

38. Who was the wicked Queen that opposed Elijah?

39. What is the most prophesied event in the Old Testament?

40. What significant event happened in the days of Peleg?

41. How old did Methuselah live to be?

42. Name the country in which Melchizedek was king.

43. Name the wife of Moses.

44. Name the Syrian army captain whom the prophet Elisha cured of leprosy.

45. For how long did Jeremiah say Israel would be held by the Babylonians?

Old Testament Answers

EASY

1. Moses
2. Samson
3. Noah
4. Jonah
5. Eve
6. Moses
7. False
8. Eve
9. The Garden of Eden
10. A pillar of salt
11. Exodus
12. Cain
13. David
14. Abraham
15. An olive leaf in a bird's mouth

AVERAGE

16. Aaron
17. Joseph
18. Genesis
19. Joshua
20. Elijah
21. Jerico
22. Solomon
23. Esau
24. Isaiah
25. See Exodus 20
26. Malachi
27. Tower of Babel
28. Sinai (Horeb)
29. Joshua
30. Jacob

HARD

31. Ham and Japheth
32. Deuteronomy
33. Abednego
34. Nebuchadnezzar
35. Naomi
36. Boaz
37. David
38. Jezebel
39. The Battle of Armageddon
40. The earth was divided
41. 969 Years
42. Salem
43. Zipporah
44. Naaman
45. 70 Years

BOOK OF MORMON
(Answers are on page 90.)

EASY

1. How many times did Moroni visit Joseph Smith the night Joseph was told about the Book of Mormon?

2. Name the descendants of Lehi who were cursed with dark skin because of their wickedness.

3. How many Book of Mormon witnesses denied they had seen the plates?

4. Name the hill where the Book of Mormon plates were buried.

5. Name the prophet who translated the Book of Mormon.

6. Name three of the sons of Lehi.

7. Name the angel who revealed to Joseph Smith the burial place of the Book of Mormon plates.

8. Did Joseph Smith's father believe him when he told him of Moroni's visitation?

9. Name the two main groups of Lehi's descendants.

10. Which of Nephi's brothers wrote one of the books of the Book of Mormon?

11. Did Christ personally visit the Nephites on this continent?

12. How many years did Joseph Smith have to wait after Moroni's visit to obtain the plates?

13. Name the father of Laman and Lemuel.

14. True or False: The sacrament was instituted by Jesus amongst the Nephites.

15. Name the servant of Laban who accompanied Lehi and his family to the promised land.

AVERAGE

16. How many men, in addition to Joseph Smith, saw the Gold Plates and gave special testimonies of it which are printed in the Book of Mormon?

17. To what man in the Book of Ether did the Savior appear as a pre-mortal spirit?

18. What is the last book in the Book of Mormon?

19. Who was the Lamanite prophet who stood on the wall and called the people to repentance?

20. What wicked city did Lehi and his family leave to migrate to America?

21. What were the people called who came to this continent from the Tower of Babel?

22. True or False: The Book of Mormon is named after the father of Mosiah.

23. What was the box made of in which Joseph Smith found the plates?

24. Who was the man who persecuted the church until being visited by an angel of the Lord?

25. What instrument did Joseph Smith use to help translate the plates?

26. What did Ammon do to the thieves who were stealing King Lamoni's sheep?

27. Name Nephi's mother.

28. Who is the author of the last book in the Book of Mormon?

29. Name the instrument that guided Lehi's family in their travels through the wilderness.

30. Which is the longest book in the Book of Mormon?

HARD

31. Name the set of plates that Lehi and his group brought to this continent which contained teachings of Moses and other Jewish Prophets.

32. Name the fourth book in the Book of Mormon.

33. Name the secret band of robbers who caused so much wickedness in the Book of Mormon.

34. Name the man who was converted by the preaching of Abinadi and who later became head of the Church.

35. Which book in the Book of Mormon contains a letter from a father to his son explaining that little children are saved without baptism?

36. What man abridged or condensed the plates of Nephi?

37. The writings of which Old Testament prophet did Jesus particularly command the Nephites to study?

38. Name the last king of the Jaredites who was discovered still living by the people of Zarahemla.

39. How long did the darkness last upon the land of the Nephites at the time of the crucifixion of Christ?

40. What group of people mentioned in the Book of Mormon migrated to this continent about the same time that Lehi and his group did?

41. Who did Nephi slay to obtain the Old Testament scriptures?

42. Which book in the Book of Mormon tells of the visit of the resurrected Christ to the Nephites?

43. What are the names of the three witnesses to the Book of Mormon?

44. What did the Lord touch to light the boats for the Jaredites as they crossed the ocean?

45. What man and his family joined Lehi and his family to journey into the wilderness?

Book of Mormon Answers

EASY

1. Three
2. Lamanites
3. None
4. Hill Cumorah
5. Joseph Smith
6. Laman, Nephi, Lemuel, Jacob, Sam, Joseph
7. Moroni
8. Yes
9. Nephites and Lamanites
10. Jacob
11. Yes
12. Four
13. Lehi
14. True
15. Zoram

AVERAGE

16. Eleven
17. Brother of Jared
18. Moroni
19. Samuel
20. Jerusalem
21. Jaredites
22. False
23. Stone
24. Alma the Younger
25. Urim and Thummim
26. Cut off their arms
27. Sariah
28. Moroni
29. Liahona (meaning a compass; also called a Ball or Director)
30. Book of Alma

HARD

31. Brass Plates of Laban
32. Enos
33. Gadianton Robbers
34. Alma
35. Moroni
36. Mormon
37. Isaiah
38. Coriantumr
39. Three days
40. Mulekites or People of Zarahemla
41. Laban
42. 3rd Nephi
43. Oliver Cowdery, David Whitmer, Martin Harris
44. 16 Stones
45. Ishmael

Church History
(Answers are on page 94.)

EASY

1. Which church did the Lord tell Joseph Smith he should join in answer to his prayers?

2. True or False: Only people who have been baptized will be resurrected.

3. What percent of one's income is a tithe?

4. True or False: Baptism is recognized by God regardless of who performs the ordinance.

5. Name the prophet who led the pioneers from Illinois to Utah.

6. What did the Lord send in order to stop crickets from destroying the crops of the pioneers in Utah?

7. True or False: Joseph Smith made a translation of parts of the Bible.

8. At what age should children be baptized?

9. Name the first, or lowest office in the Aaronic Priesthood.

10. What is the revelation called that advises us not to use tobacco or strong drinks?

11. Name the town and state where the first LDS temple was built.

12. How many distinct and separate personages are there in the Godhead?

13. Name the four books recognized as scripture by The Church of Jesus Christ of Latter-day Saints.

14. How many years is a millennium?

15. True or False: Adam held the higher or Melchizedek Priesthood.

AVERAGE

16. True or False: Adam was never baptized.

17. How many degrees of glory are there in the heavens?

18. True or False: A teacher in the Aaronic Priesthood has the power and authority to baptize.

19. True or False: The spirits of all men and women are the literal offspring of God.

20. Name the brother of Joseph Smith who was appointed to be a Patriarch to the Church.

21. Upon the death of the President of the Church, which body of men is the directing authority in the Church?

22. Name the personage who restored the Aaronic Priesthood to the earth in the latter days.

23. Give the names of the three kingdoms or degrees of glory in order, from the highest to the lowest.

24. Name six heavenly personages which appeared to Joseph Smith during the restoration of the gospel.

25. Name the three heavenly messengers who restored the Melchizedek Priesthood to Joseph Smith.

26. Who was the President of the Church following Heber J. Grant?

27. Name the fourth President of The Church of Jesus Christ of Latter-day Saints.

28. What ward officer is president of the Aaronic Priesthood?

29. In what year did Joseph Smith receive his first vision ?

30. How many members did it take to organize The Church of Jesus Christ of Latter-day Saints?

HARD

31. Name the city in which the second LDS Temple was constructed.

32. How many members does it take to compose a full quorum of elders?

33. Name the man who organized the first Sunday School after the pioneers arrived in Utah.

34. Name four men of the original Quorum of Twelve in The Church of Jesus Christ of Latter-day Saints.

35. Which President of the Church is remembered for bringing the Church out of financial bondage by teaching the law of tithing?

36. Name the first Presiding Patriarch to the church.

37. Name the temple in which Moses, Elijah, and Elias appeared and restored certain keys of the priesthood.

38. Name the particular covenant or ordinance that a person must enter into to have the blessing of eternal increase of spirit children in the hereafter.

39. Name the brother of Joseph Smith who was one of the first missionaries in the Church and whose labor indirectly brought the gospel to Brigham Young.

40. Name the man who was wounded in the Carthage jail at the time of the martyrdom of Joseph Smith, and who later became President of the Church.

41. True or False: God has created other worlds besides the one we live on.

42. True or False: Persons who aren't baptized while living on earth are forever lost and can never enter the Kingdom of God.

43. What name was Adam also known by?

44. Which of the Standard Works of the Church is divided into sections rather than chapters?

45. On a piece of paper, write the name of the Church. Spell, capitalize and punctuate it correctly.

Church History Answers

EASY

1. None of them
2. False
3. Ten percent
4. False
5. Brigham Young
6. Sea gulls
7. True
8. Eight
9. Deacon
10. Word of Wisdom
11. Kirtland, Ohio
12. Three
13. Bible, Book of Mormon, Pearl of Great Price, Doctrine & Covenants
14. One Thousand
15. True

AVERAGE

16. False (Moses 6:64-65)
17. Three
18. False
19. True
20. Hyrum Smith

21. The Quorum of the Twelve Apostles
22. John the Baptist
23. Celestial, Terrestrial, Telestial
24. God the Father, Jesus, Moroni, John the Baptist, Peter, James, John, Moses, Elias and Elijah
25. Peter, James, John
26. George Albert Smith
27. Wilford Woodruff
28. Bishop
29. 1820
30. Six

HARD

31. Nauvoo, Illinois
32. 96 Members
33. Richard Ballantyne

34. Thomas B. Marsh, David W. Patten, Brigham Young, Heber Kimball, Orson Pratt, Wm. Mclellen, Parley P. Pratt, Luke Johnson, Wm. Smith, Orson Hyde, Lyman Johnson
35. Lorenzo Snow
36. Joseph Smith, Sr.
37. Kirtland, Ohio
38. Marriage for Time and Eternity
39. Samuel H. Smith
40. John Taylor
41. True
42. False
43. Michael
44. The Doctrine & Covenants
45. The Church of Jesus Christ of Latter-day Saints

Index